Show Me the Light

Melissa Cizik

Preface

I started writing poetry at a very difficult time in my life. I was 19 and struggling with my mental health in college. Unfortunately, I felt unable to speak or connect with my friends and family about the emotional pain that I was in. When I mustered the courage to go to therapy, I was unable to fully open up to my therapist. One day my therapist suggested that I write down my thoughts. In that way, I was able to express myself fully. Overtime, I associated writing with the comfort and emotional release I had received in therapy. I continued writing whenever I was in distress. As time went on, I started turning my writings into poetry. Eventually, I was able to talk to my therapist about the trauma that I went through. My mental health kept improving. Show Me the Light is a guide to my healing journey and how I used spirituality, faith, mindfulness, nature, and shadow work to heal my body, mind, and spirit. My hope is that this book gives you the same guidance, comfort, and understanding that writing poetry has given me.

The Things that are Fleeing

The spirituality of me
Has come from a constant need to leave
To leave this body
To leave this world
The spirituality of myself
Of this being
Has been born
From extreme time in the darkness
The spirituality of me
Has been birthed
By myself
From a constant search for light

Consciousness

Who am I?
And what does this mean?
How did I become?
The snake in the garden
Was just a part of me
Me wanting to understand myself
To gain the knowledge
And eat the fruit
To feel it flowing down my throat
Of what it means to be
To exist to an entirety
To eat it up
To be alive
To be aware
To be myself
Means to understand the darkness
To be me means to be corrupted
To be selfish
To go against
To revolt
To suffer
To be me means
To have the knowledge
And still choose to do good

The Silence gets Loud

My screams
Are stuck in my brain
Entangled in my thoughts
Echoing in me for days
Bouncing from left to right
They can't find their way to my mouth
My screams make no noise
They get stuck in thought

Frozen

Winter is coming
The winds start to eat up my flesh
And my blood turns cold
I have ice running through my blood
Affecting my thoughts
No understanding
A frozen brain
Unable to remember the warmth that came with august
No rational thoughts
How bizarre
to have icicles hanging all the way down to my throat
No contribution can be pulled out of me
I am in iceberg
Taking up space in my own body

Flesh and Blood

Despite the drive to better myself
At the end of the day
I have to comply with my body
My anatomy
Has control
I spend my life
Trying to heal
What I didn't brake
Because that's the contract I signed up for
To have a body and live in it
To bear the constraints
That come with being human

Authenticity

The thing about healing was
That it could toke a lifetime
And it often did
But the process could only start
By surrendering
To being completely yourself

Warmth

It is sunlight on my skin
Transcending into my blood
Moving through my being
It is me
In you
And you
In me
It is the flow of life
In invincible bloodline
Connecting all of us
Flowing through the universe
Flowing through me
And through you

An Instrument

It comes out out of my core
And this is the tool I use to convey it to you
It feels like comfort
Like all of my sufferings have been lifted off
Like I am floating among the clouds
But me and the clouds are one
So no one will ever be able to separate us
Because it is not possible
I am not in it
I am a part of it
And my body is being used to play the music
The notes are the letters
And my soul is the conductor

Chilling Sounds

The winds start to cry
Like the ghost of woman
Who have been locked up in the air
And are screaming to be released from the atmosphere
They cry to warn us
Of the life they wished they could have learned to live
They cry because they know all the ugly that the world has
But they miss being able to feel the beauty

24K

No wrong
No past
No mental illness
Could ever get in the way
Of your dreams
If you have the type of heart that is pure
Because God has shielded you
You walk around with the greatest force that there is
And because of that
You have been protected
Shielded in the highest type of gold
In God's touch

Eyes of the Heart

The heart transcends any sense
Deeply rooted in our existence
Speaking in scripture
Crying in verses
And rejoicing in truth
The window to the core
The control center to our being
Screaming to be accepted
To be welcomed in its own home
To be purified with your love

Flow

The swirling of the current of life
Has no start or end
The force is driven entirely by the unknown
How strange
To be a part of something
And not know why it made you
To have to question what created you
To ask for the purpose and meaning
Only to be left in silence
And to have to make it up yourself
Whatever it is
A cycle of death
And birth
Continuously flowing through space
A make up of what we call life

Autumn

The wind comes
And the leaves start dancing
They start fluttering together
In sync
Singing and rustling to the chorus of nature
What in act to witness

Gloss of Hope

Why do you do it
What is it that you see
You look at the sky
And you get stuck in this dream
In this idea of yourself
That you can't live up to
Because you don't have the courage to be
To have it kill you
To let it make you a new
So what do you do
You fill yourself with substance
Because it's the only way you will see it
In those glistening eyes
I can see myself

What the Water Gave Me

Drip on to it
Until all the droplets have melted into each other
No more division exist within you
You have been integrated into life
Fallen from the sky
It is water
Essential to your being
You need water to help
With the division that exist in you
Let your full being melt into yourself
Like droplets of rain merging into a puddle
It is the only way you will be complete

Make Me Come

Remind me of where I come from
Or where im gonna go
Remind me
Of the place
That nothing lives
Just everyone we know
Remind me

Dream Woman

I was in a home
With someone who loved me
I was on a cloud
Floating in the idea
I was happy
The world was tinted in red
And it emanated reason and purpose
I walked with the wisdom
That someone created this world
For one reason
So that I could love myself

Running Towards Myself

The deeper I'm in the woods
The deeper I'm in myself
My soul is at home
And the trees are feeding me authenticity

Show Me the Light

My skin is burning
In discomfort
In pain
In uneasiness
But I need it to grow
I need the fire to burn off all my skin
So that I can have a new set
I am on fire
And it hurts good
I need this
This hurt will help me grow
It will create a light
That I will always remember
Because I feel it
Burn it all off
Fire
give me fire

The Fruits

I can see your roots
The things that contribute to your growth
The things that made you
I can see the soil that nourished you
And the pesticides they put on you
Because I have been chosen to feel
To bear the fruits
To watch them fall off
And be used as fertilizer
For the soil that holds us all

Integrating the Shadow

I swallowed my sufferings
And ate them
And when they were in me
I had to watch them
Feed them
Take them on a walk
Nourish them
I had to lock them up
So they wouldn't eat me
And even then
I couldnt get rid of it
It was a part of me
Engraved into me
Waiting for me to make a mistake
So it could eat me up from the inside
How could it be that I was causing all of it
How could I create a demon so controlling
That I could not recognize myself at times
Over time I brought it out
I took it to therapy with me
It turned beautiful
When I learned to love it
To nurture it
I gave it kisses and hugs
And it loved me back
I was no longer housing a demon `
I was loving myself
All the parts of me

Now and Forever

I am living in the future and the past
I exist at all times
They call it a present
Everything gets created here
Like an infinite rotation of energy
Everything is happening at once

It Keeps Going

The wheel never stops
Attached to something infinite
An invincible force moving the wheels of life
The only way you can begin to understand it
Is if you hop on
But it moves up in a different vibration
So listen

The Heliocentric Understanding

The level of understanding
That comes from experience
And many lives
The type that you intuitively accept
From the things you have felt
Because the things you have endured
Have caused you to understand it all
That despite the harm
And evil that exist in the world of men
The rays always came out of their core
That despite the wrong they did
They always had a choice to center themselves
The understanding that keeps the world spinning
The ultimate understanding

The Flame

You have reached
My center
A ripple of energy
That Is me
And you
Together
Us

Keep it

Let it marinate
And let my words
Absorb into your deepest cell
Let me be the one to tell you
That we are connected
By the garden
That connects us all
We belong to the same seed

Us Against the Underworld

Bring your demons to me
Tell me what is bothering you
So I can poor love on them
So you don't have to fight them yourself
Bring your demons to me
So I can tell them
Just how much
I love you

To Create

To have
The infinite
In you
Is to have this
Endless knowledge
That never stops spinning

Soul Lines?

I look at the lines on your inner palm
And I see my own
Every break on your skin
Is bound to happen in mine
We are connected by something invincible
A delusion in my head

All at Once

It dances out of my skin
And kisses the air
It guides the birds in flight
Connecting each and everyone
It grounds the trees
And goes down to the sea
Until it reaches the stars
And comes right back to me

To Existence,

    I wrote the poems for you.

Home

You feel like that place
That is not a place
That state
That lives
Uncontaminated
That constant flow
That surpasses all of it
You are a part
Of my nothingness
That is everything
The silence
Where thoughts do not exist
The core of it all
The circle of the beginning
And the end
That we call eternity

It Turned Out

Fixing my life
Was always something
That I had to do internally
That the war could only be ended If I figured out
Where both sides were coming from
That someone else did not have to validate me
That I could only validate myself
That the love that I wanted
Could only be made by me

Spectrum

The good can not be good
Without the infusion of the bad
The scale
Measures the balance
Of the polar opposites
Each giving birth
To each other
Creating the infinite

The Cave

Fall into your heart
It is going to be a deep ride
This is your connection to the gods
The deeper you fall
The greater the outcome will be
Surrender into yourself
To get out
You have to go deeper
Face yourself
And your demons
Face your truth

A Bouquet of Metaphors

This blooms from my death
This gives life to the pain
That killed me
This resurrects me
With no body
On earth
This connects me
To where I came from
To the nothingness that made me
To the nothingness I go

An Eventful Time

What was I doing in my 20s?
 I was crying.

Affirm it

What I think
I am
When thoughts start to invade
I turn to repetition
I start
Unraveling the knot
Of misunderstanding
That has overstayed
In my mind
I start to ground myself
In who I am

Thank You

Give thanks
And you will receive it all
But first you must accept
You must feel it
In your bones
Rushing through your blood
Pumping in your heart
You must be filed
With the knowledge that life
Is a gift

Crystalized

The frequency emitted
From a crystal
Can assist
In the healing
In the forgiving
In the grounding
Of yourself
They get the point
You are who you are
No matter what

Forgiveness

The only way to break the cycle
Of ancestral trauma
Is to forgive
To forgive all those that came before you
In order
To heal the genes
You have to understand
That it was carried down
For a purpose
And that you would probably do the same
As those that did to you
If you only had the tools they had
That the separation of your bodies, shame and guilt
Was all a lie
That we are all the same body
Experiencing itself
Over and over
Until you have
Understood
And forgiven
First yourself
Then the other versions of you

The Simulation

The people in your life
When you are young
Make your program
Whatever is happening in their lives
Will continually happen in yours
To break out of the cycle
Of the matrix of your genes
You heal
Forgive
And you rise
By loving yourself
You are free

The Fall

The first have started changing
Showing the rest of us
That it is time
To say goodbye to the leaves
That we have raised
It is time to have them fall
Let us be your reminder
That life is a constant cycle
Of death
And rebirth
That the revolution
Can not be complete
Without something coming to an end

The Flower of Life

This is temporary
There is a circle of completeness
That we all originate from
Try not to get stuck in this world
And live everyday like you are on a trip
What a blessing
To wake up with the realization
That the human experience is just that
An experience

Made up of the Universe

The intensity of our feelings
Illuminates the secrets that made us
It is all in our experiences
The good and the bad
Everything is made up of us

Filled to the Top

The cup overflows
When you know it is much bigger than you
When you give yourself
When you surrender

Remember

Love is the ultimate revelation
Love is the string between the darkness of our past
And the beauty of our present
It is us represented in everything else
It is God in us
And the world around us
In all forms
Love is it
It is all of it

Quantum Entanglement

Most days I sit at the bottom of eternity
With the weight of my life
And everyone else's life In my heart
I listen to the duality
That the waves make
In sound and in movement
Most days I have watched my life past me many times
Unable to change the intricate set of lines
That connect our paths
Most days I watch the ocean
Inside of the clouds
Inside of our world
Inside of my head

True Love

The greatest love story you will ever witness
Is the one where you fall in love with yourself

Sacred Geometry

The underlying
The fundamentals
Of everything
Can be tied to one thought
One idea
The concept of
Pure Love

The Divine Feminine

Receives all of it
The God of our existence
My mom
My earth
My universe

The Breath

Your lungs expand and contract
Like the feathers of a bird
Learn to control
Your breath
And you can reach the sky
Only when
You have mastered the flow
Of your own wings
Can you enter
The kingdom of heaven

The Recognition

I am not flawed
I am not broken
I am perfect
My experiences have not defined me
I have stayed a constant
Uncontaminated
I have stayed myself
I have stayed whole

Free

The liberation of accepting yourself Is priceless
I suggest you spend all the time you need in healing
In holding space for yourself
You spend a lot of time on earth
And it does not have to be hell
Free yourself of anything that does not belong to you

The True Mechanism of Healing

It is done in work
It is done in energy
It is done with the knowledge
that you might never heal
But the work still has to done
There are two forces
Always emerging in each other
Fighting to win
Which side will you contribute to?

The Fabrication of my Dreams

I have written these words
woven in joy and pain
I meticulously chose this path
To heal my inner child
I have created something beautiful
Of everything that has broken me
I have learned the duality of life
I have produced my very own American Dream

We Rise Together

The shift takes place
When we have all risen
When we have all as a collective
Gained the wisdom
That comes with pain
Until we have gained the freedom
That comes with surrendering
Surrendering to the greatest good
For humanity
For us all

The Universal Consciousness

There is a field
Where I can be myself
I collapsed into my being
And Jumped into the void
Traveling down
My body was turned into dust
All the atoms and particles that I called me
Were stretched out into existence
I questioned nothing
Existence is beautiful and colorful
This is where the light lives
Myself is good
Myself is pure
Because I am here
Speaking to you
As existence

Made in the USA
Middletown, DE
21 March 2023

27307808R00038